AF334198

CLASSICAL REPERTOIRE FOR TRUMPET

TRUMPET SOLO/VOLUME TWO

ARRANGED BY COSTEL PUSCOIU

Free piano accompaniment available online!
Visit: www.melbay.com/98192

CLASSICAL REPERTOIRE FOR TRUMPET

CONTENTS

VOLUME TWO

FOREWORD

In 1991 I brought out the first edition of my CLASSICAL REPERTOIRE FOR PAN PIPES. Now I present CLASSICAL REPERTOIRE FOR TRUMPET in B flat with piano accompaniments. This work contains music which I adapted and arranged especially for the trumpet. In my opinion classical music is the best basis for learning to play any instrument.

Great performers have proven that the trumpet can be successfully used for playing not only classic music, but also symphonic or chamber music form classical, romantic or modern period just as well as any other musical instrument. No longer is the contemporary repertoire considered unfit for the trumpet.

Every sincere instrumentalist needs a regular study program. Daily practice of technical exercises and etudes is necessary for improving and maintaining the acquired results. Regularly playing works of music should be the aim of every musician, amateur as well as professional.

It has not been easy to find suitable and nice music for all levels. It was especially difficult to find simple melodies. I think that for the beginning player studying well–known melodies is both easy and enjoyable. I have carefully chosen the best keys for violin and therefore many songs are not in the keys in which they were originally written. Also a number of other adaptations have been introduced to make the music more suitable for performance on the trumpet in B flat. The structure of the music has not been altered.

I hope you will find my CLASSICAL REPERTOIRE FOR TRUMPET not only instructive and useful, but also pleasant and entertaining. Lots of success.

Costel Puscoiu

ABOUT THE AUTHOR

Costel Puscoiu was born on August 29, 1951, in Bucharest, Romania. He studied and graduated at the "Ciprian Porumbescu" College of Music in Bucharest, majoring in "Composition and Theory". In Romania he worked as a music teacher, and for some years he was a conductor and researcher at the Institute for Ethnology and Folklore in Bucharest. He was also a member of the Society of Romanian Composers.

His compositions comprise symphonic music (symphony, cantatas, concerto for viola), chamber music (string quartets, sonata for clarinet and piano, contemporary for several ensembles, pieces of music for pan flute), choir pieces, and film scores. His compositions are often influenced by Romanian folklore and Byzantine liturgies. His hand has also appeared in several musicological and folkloric studies and articles.

In September of 1982 he preferred The Netherlands to his native Romania; now he's working in the music school department as a pan flute teacher and a leader of an orchestra at "The Free Academy Westvest" in Delft. Meanwhile he has become a member of the Dutch Composers Association.

Minuet

(*from* Sonata No. 2 in B Minor)

Johann Sebastian Bach

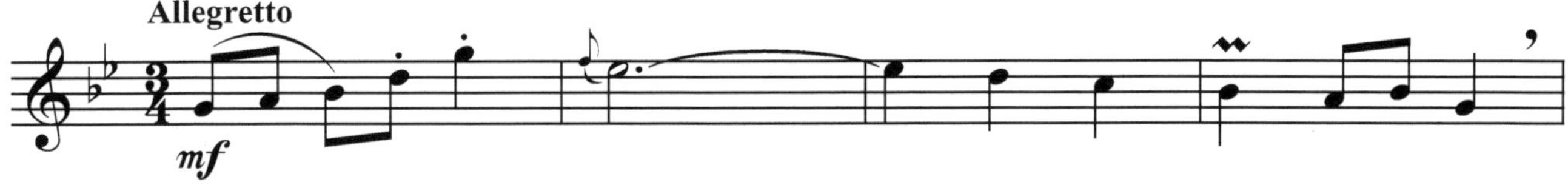

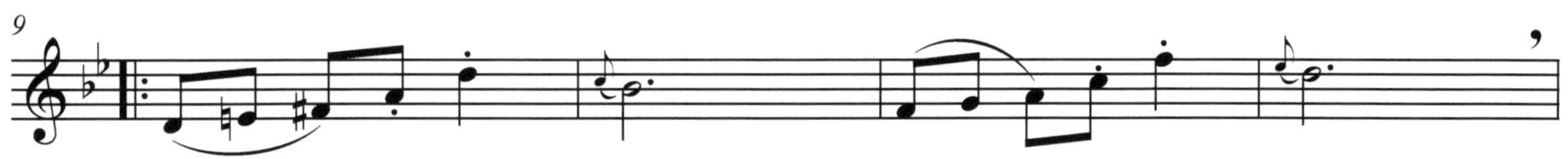

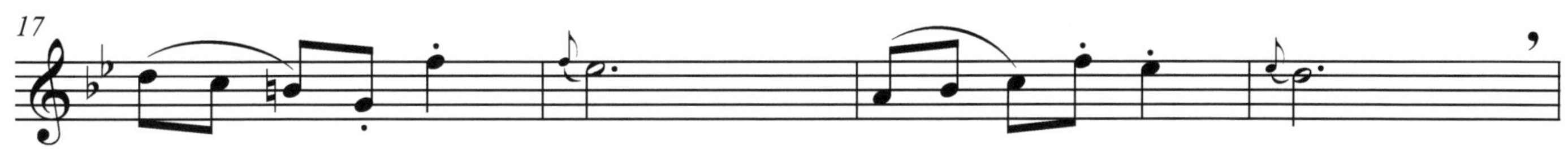

Scherzo

(*from* Symphony No. 2)

Johannes Brahms

Etude

(Op. 10, No. 3)

Frederic Chopin

Rondeau

Espirit Philippe Chedeville

March of the Hunters

(*from* Opera "Der Freischütz")

Carl Maria Von Weber

9

Theme from "Winter"

(*from* "The Four Seasons")

Antonio Vivaldi

Are You With Me

Adagio

(*from* Sonata E Minor)

Francesco Geminiani

Andante

(*from* Piano Concerto No. 21 in C Major)

Wolfgang Amadeus Mozart

Vlad's Song

Costel Puscoiu

Allemanda

(*from* Sonata in A Minor)

Arcangelo Corelli

This page has been left blank
to avoid awkward page turns.

Allegro

(*from* Sonata No. 2 in A Minor)

Diogenio Bigaglia

Vivace

(*from* Sonata in E Minor)

Francesco Geminiani

Trumpet Voluntary

Bourree

(*from* Suite No. 2 in B Minor)

Johann Sebastian Bach

Allegro

Wolfgang Amadeus Mozart

Moment Musical

(Op. 94, No. 3)

Franz Schubert

Rejoicing

(*from* "Fireworks Music")

Georg Friedrich Händel

Polonaise

(*from* Suite No. 2 in B Minor)

Johann Sebastian Bach

Allegro Giocoso

(*from* Sonata "La Persane")

Philbert de Lavigne

Ouverture

(*from* Suite No. 2 in B Minor)

Johann Sebastian Bach

In the Hall of the Mountain King

(*from* "Peer Gynt")

Edvard Grieg

This page has been left blank
to avoid awkward page turns.

Alla Hornpipe

(*from* "Water Music")

Georg Friedrich Händel

28

40
mf
43
leggiero
(,)
46
(,)
49
tr
tr
(,) tr
52
(,)
56
leggiero
(,)
59
(,)
62
(,)
65
tr
68
(,)
71
D.S. al Fine
(,)
tr

Serenade

(*from* String Quartet No. 17 in F Major)

Joseph Haydn

Andante cantabile

p dolce

Ave Maria

Allegretto Grazioso

(*from* Sonata "La Persane")

Philbert de Lavigne

Rondeau

(*from* Suite No. 2 in B Minor)

Johann Sebastian Bach

Allegretto

mf mf p mf p mf p mf mf

Minuet in G

Ludwig Van Beethoven
Tempo di minuetto lento
Trio
piu mosso
Fine
D.C. al Fine

Slavonic Dance

(Op. 46, No. 4)

Antonin Dvořák

28
A tempo
f
32
p
pp
36
cresc. molto
f
fp
40
dim.
pp
43
p
cresc. molto
ff
46
50
fz
fz
54
fz
fz
ff

Solvejg's Song

(from "Peer Gynt")

Edvard Grieg

Sinfonia

(*from* Cantata No. 156)

Johann Sebastian Bach

The Swan

(*from* "Le Carnaval des Animaux")

Camille Saint–Saëns

This page has been left blank
to avoid awkward page turns.

Pavane

Gabriel Fauré

Allegro

(*from* Brandenburg Concerto No. 5)

Johann Sebastian Bach

The Peace

(*from* "Fireworks Music")

Georg Friedrich Händel

Allegro

(*from* Brandenburg Concerto No. 1)

Johann Sebastian Bach

Romance

(*from* "Eine Kleine Nachtmusik")

Wolfgang Amadeus Mozart

46

BILL'S
MUSIC
SHELF
UNIQUELY INTERESTING MUSIC!